NICK HUNTER

ILLUSTRATED BY
EOIN COVENEY

GREAT PIONEERS

Contents

What it takes to be a pioneer	2
Pioneers of television	4
Emmeline Pankhurst	9
Amelia Earhart	16
Frank Whittle	24
Clarence Birdseye	29
Jacques Piccard	35
Nelson Mandela	40
More great pioneers	46
Glossary and index	48

OXFORD
UNIVERSITY PRESS

Watermore
Levelled Readers

What it takes to be a pioneer

We're going to explore what it takes to be a pioneer.

Pioneers are trailblazers. But being one isn't always easy …

Leslie Mitchell and Elizabeth Cowell were pioneers. They were the first ever television presenters.

You need determination.

A pioneer could be the first person to visit somewhere that no one's ever been before.

Only another 300 metres more to go!

Oh no, I thought we were already at the top!

You need to be inventive …

A pioneer might make something that changes the world.

… and tenacious.

So you keep going when things go wrong.

A pioneer can be someone who discovers something new.

You might need to be brave.

Nice, err, gorilla?

A pioneer might work to solve a problem or change people's views in order to make the world a better place.

You think you've found a cure for hayfever? Well done!

Aaaa-chooo!

Maybe it needs a little more work.

You're right, Leslie. Being a pioneer is tough.

Sometimes you also need a bit of luck.

We were in the right place at the right time – at the very start of television broadcasting. Let us tell you our story.

Pioneers of television

There were many pioneers in television ...

Not least the man who started it all ...

In 1926, John Logie Baird invented the first television system.

You'll be able to send moving pictures into people's homes. I call it television.

Impressive, but I can't see it catching on.

In 1934, at the British Broadcasting Corporation (BBC) ...

So, we're agreed. Television is the sort of thing the BBC should be doing.

Up until this point the BBC had only been responsible for radio broadcasting. Television was something very different. It needed new skills and knowledge.

Congratulations, Gerald! You're the new Director of Television.

We've got four months until we send out our first live broadcast. We need to find some television presenters!

WANTED:
Television presenters
Applicants must have:
- Charm
- Clear voice
- Cool head in a crisis

Apply to: Director of Television, BBC

"Television presenter auditions. Next please!"

"There are hundreds of people here. I've got no chance!"

Each candidate had to do a screen test.

"I think we've decided, don't you?"

"Elizabeth Cowell has the right mix of charm and style."

"Leslie Mitchell will be perfect. He can talk about nothing-in-particular brilliantly!"

5

Alexandra Palace in London was the home of the BBC's new television service.

The first television programmes were due to be broadcast in November 1936.

However, some test programmes were needed for a special exhibition.

The Radiolympia exhibition was a chance for manufacturers to demonstrate their TV sets to the public ... and they needed test programmes for this.

Nine days?

We need programmes in nine days' time!

On 26th August 1936, Elizabeth became the first TV presenter.

Hello ... This is direct television broadcasting from the studios at Alexandra Palace.

That's the test done. Next time it will be the real thing.

Before the first official broadcast, engineers checked the new equipment was working.

Lights and cameras had to be positioned.

Singers and musicians had to rehearse.

On 2nd November 1936, at 3pm, around a hundred television sets were switched on across London for viewers to watch the first television broadcasts.

Picture Page was the first regular show on television, hosted by Leslie and Elizabeth.

Good afternoon, ladies and gentlemen ...

So that's the story of how we became pioneers – the world's first TV stars.

Let's find out about some other pioneers ...

7

Television facts

Timeline of UK television

1922 The British Broadcasting Corporation is formed to ensure a single body responsible for radio broadcasts in the UK.

1925 John Logie Baird first transmits a moving television picture in his laboratory.

1926 John demonstrates his improved equipment publically for the first time.

1928 John transmits a television signal across the Atlantic and demonstrates colour television.

1929 The first television trials by the BBC.

1936 The BBC officially launches its first regular television service.

1938 The first television news bulletin is broadcast.

1937 The first live sports event is broadcast at a specially arranged football match between Arsenal and Arsenal Reserves.

1939 Television service shut down due to the Second World War.

1946 Television service resumes following the war and soon includes special children's programmes for the first time.

1949 The first televised weather forecast is broadcast.

1953 The coronation of Queen Elizabeth II is watched by around 20 million viewers. This marks the beginning in a rise in TV ownership among the general public.

1954 A new channel, ITV, is given licence to broadcast.

1960 The first TV soap opera, *Coronation Street*, is broadcast on ITV.

1964 BBC2 airs for the first time.

1969 BBC1 and ITV now broadcast in colour.

1982 Channel 4 first broadcasts.

1989 The first satellite television channels are broadcast.

1998 The first digital television service is launched.

2012 All analogue services are finally switched off, meaning a choice between digital and satellite options and many more television stations are now available to everyone.

Emmeline Pankhurst

This pioneer had a real battle on her hands; she wanted to make life better for millions of women.

Emmeline Pankhurst spent her whole life fighting for justice ...

... and was even arrested for her beliefs.

You are under arrest, Mrs Pankhurst!

Emmeline grew up when Queen Victoria was on the throne. At the time, no woman could vote in elections. Her family believed this was wrong.

Father, why are the members of parliament always men?

Because our society is not equal. Women cannot vote so they cannot be members of parliament.

Where are you going, Mother?

There's a meeting about votes for women.

Can I come too?

This must change! I will not stop striving for change until women can vote.

Votes for women!

Even when she was older and had children of her own, Emmeline continued campaigning.

Emmeline campaigned her whole life.

Votes for women!

You've been organizing meetings for years, Mother, but we are no closer to getting the vote.

You're right – there must be a better way.

Manchester, 1903 ...

Welcome to the first meeting of the Women's Social and Political Union.

What can we do that hasn't been tried before?

Our plan is simple – deeds, not words.

Women's Social and Political Union (WSPU) members started disrupting political meetings.

Will the government give votes to women?

Be quiet, or we'll call the police!

WSPU members were not scared to go to prison if it got them noticed.

Hundreds of women have joined us since we started disrupting meetings.

The newspapers have started calling us **suffragettes**.

10

On 19th February 1906, the first suffragette protest march in London …

"Equal rights for women!"

"Only a new government will bring change. We cannot vote, but we can speak out!"

In February 1908, a group of suffragettes marched on Parliament. Emmeline led the protest herself.

"Votes for women!"
"Votes for women!"
"Votes for women!"

Emmeline was arrested for obstruction after trying to enter Parliament.

"Take your hands off me!"

"This court finds you guilty. Keep the peace or go to prison for six weeks."

"I choose prison."

"You can't have any visitors or letters for the first month."

11

March 1908: Emmeline is freed from her first prison sentence.

"This is a terrible place, but prison will not stop our movement."

On 21st June 1908, there was a rally in Hyde Park, London ...

"There must be 500 000 people here, but still the Government won't listen!"

"What if the government keeps ignoring us, Mother?"

"We will *make* them listen!"

Emmeline and her followers started causing more trouble. They broke windows ...

"Votes for women!"

... chased government ministers ... and set fire to buildings and postboxes.

"The suffragettes are at it again. Damaging the Minister's car."

"Does Mrs Pankhurst think she can win with this behaviour?"

"Will the men in power imprison us all?"

"If they lock up hundreds of respectable women, many people will side with us."

The more women that were arrested, the more people heard about their cause.

The suffragettes found a new way to protest.

"The suffragettes won't follow prison orders, and they refuse to eat any food."

Emmeline went on **hunger strike** many times in prison.

"Another delicious meal for you, Mrs Pankhurst!"

When the hunger strikers became too weak, the authorities were sometimes forced to release them.

Even Emmeline's daughters sometimes disagreed with her ideas ...

"Many women are put off supporting us by these violent attacks."

"I'm the leader and you MUST support me."

"I didn't know it was a crime to disagree."

"I don't care if Sylvia and Adela desert me. Our cause is what matters, Christabel."

In August 1914 ...

BRITAIN AT WAR WITH GERMANY

"We will never be able to vote if Britain is defeated!"

"The men will be fighting, but women also demand the right to serve our country."

Women took on many new jobs during World War One.

In 1918, when the war ended, women over thirty were finally allowed to vote.

POLLING STATION

"Emmeline Pankhurst was the first campaigner who encouraged women to fight for themselves."

"She was a true pioneer."

Emmeline Pankhurst facts

- Emmeline was born in Manchester on 14th July 1858, into a family with a history of radical politics. When she was twenty-one, she married Richard Pankhurst, who was a big supporter of the suffrage movement.
- She was the founder of the Women's Social and Political Union (WSPU) and leader of the suffragette movement.
- She was arrested on many occasions. The suffragettes' decision to hunger strike led to the government introducing a new act whereby prisoners who wouldn't eat were released and then rearrested once they had recovered.
- After World War One, Emmeline and Christabel opened a tea shop in southern France. Sadly their new career was not a success.
- Emmeline died on 14th June 1928. Shortly after, women were finally granted equal voting rights with men (they were allowed to vote at the age of twenty-one).
- In her own words: "[To bring about change] you have to make more noise than anybody else … in fact you have to be there all the time and see that they do not snow you under."

Emmeline Pankhurst
British Suffragette leader
14th July 1858–
14th June 1928

Amelia Earhart

Our next pioneer showed that women could reach for the sky.

"Amelia, how does it feel to be a record-breaking pilot?"

"It's great to prove that a woman can fly just as well as any man."

"When did you know you wanted to be a pilot?"

"I was always fascinated by planes, but it wasn't until I had my first ride that I became hooked."

1920, California.

"Wow! I wonder what it would be like to fly one of those."

Amelia's father took her to an air show.

She even got to have her first trip in a plane.

"This is magical!"

Later ...

"I think I'd like to fly."

"Are you sure?"

"We can't afford flying lessons."

"Oh Dad, please! I'll get a job."

"OK, but you'll have to find an instructor."

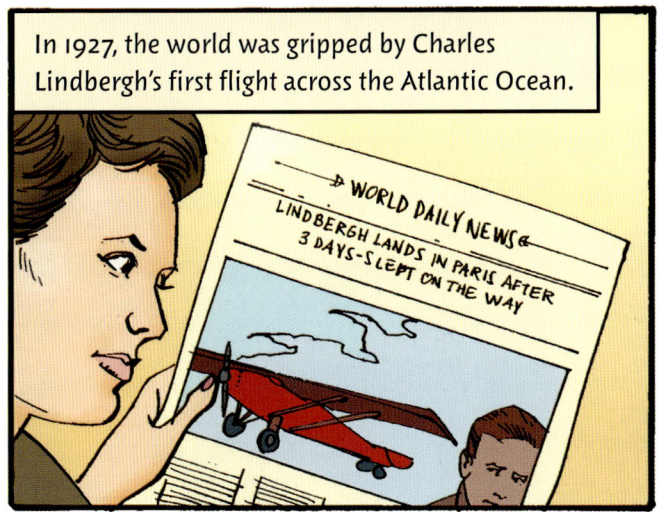

"Dad, this is Anita Snook, my flying instructor."

Eventually, Amelia saved up enough to buy her first aircraft.

In 1927, the world was gripped by Charles Lindbergh's first flight across the Atlantic Ocean.

WORLD DAILY NEWS
LINDBERGH LANDS IN PARIS AFTER 3 DAYS - SLEPT ON THE WAY

Boston, 1928 ...

"Hello, Miss Earhart. I'm George Putnam. I have an exciting project for you. Would you like to be the first woman to cross the Atlantic by air?"

Amelia was selected for the flight, alongside experienced male pilots Wilmer Stutz and Slim Gordon.

"We need to wait for a good forecast."

"But what if another woman crosses the Atlantic before I do?"

17

Amelia's journal: 17th June 1928, our flight begins.

Finally we're on our way.

Next stop Europe!

18th June, midnight: It's extremely cold and damp. We are wearing fur-lined flying suits.

18th June, dawn: We're flying low to use wind and save fuel. Worried about engines cutting out.

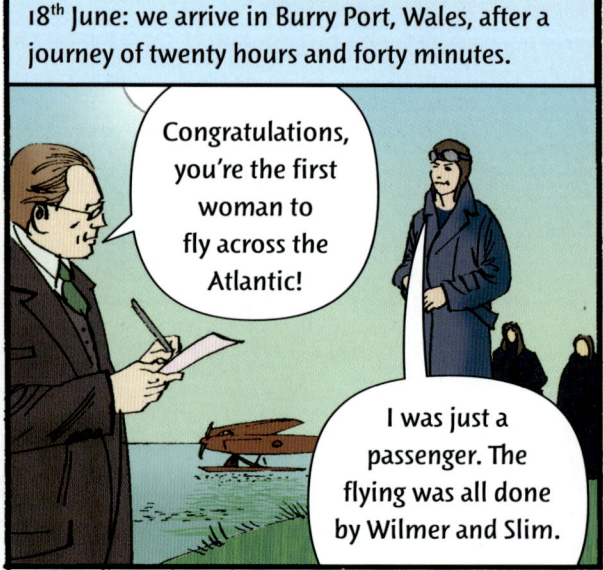

18th June, 8am: Ships seen below – land must be close. We're very low on fuel.

I can see land on the horizon. We might just make it!

18th June: we arrive in Burry Port, Wales, after a journey of twenty hours and forty minutes.

Congratulations, you're the first woman to fly across the Atlantic!

I was just a passenger. The flying was all done by Wilmer and Slim.

18

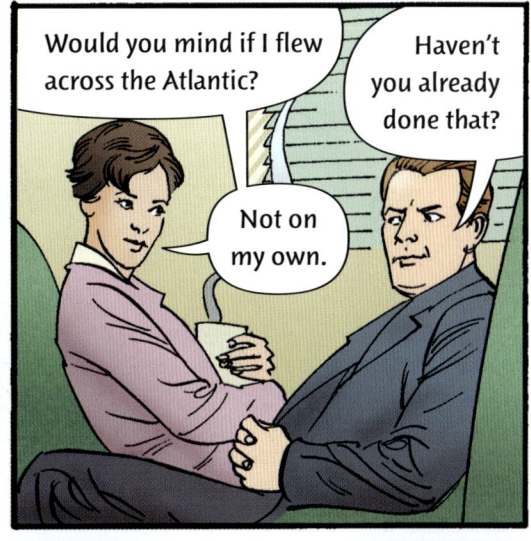

George Putnam sold Amelia's story to make her famous.

They were married in 1931.

"Would you mind if I flew across the Atlantic?"

"Haven't you already done that?"

"Not on my own."

Amelia's next trip across the Atlantic was planned in secret.

"Why keep quiet about it?"

"There's a risk someone might get there before me."

"Do you think you can do it? It's very dangerous."

"I know the risks. There's nowhere to land in an emergency. My aircraft and my **navigation** will have to be perfect."

"It needs a new engine, and it will have to be strengthened."

"I'm not letting you go unless the weather is perfect."

"So how's the weather looking?"

"Just sit tight and wait!"

Amelia left for Canada to make preparations.

20th May 1932, Harbour Grace, Newfoundland ...

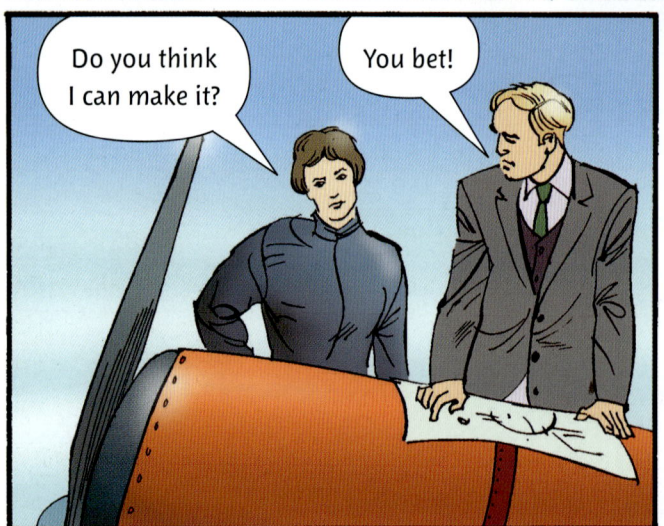

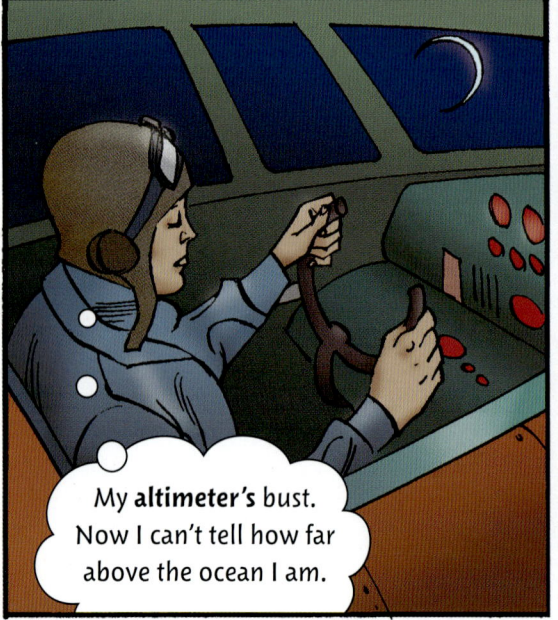

It's your husband. He says it's urgent!

There's a slot of clear weather, but it may not last. How soon can you leave?

This afternoon.

Do you think I can make it?

You bet!

So long Amelia!

Good luck!

My **altimeter's** bust. Now I can't tell how far above the ocean I am.

Amelia's journal: 20th May, evening: Flying through fierce storm. May have been knocked off course.

21st May, midnight: Damage to exhaust. Can see flames. Tempted to turn back but too late now.

21st May, early morning: Climbing to avoid clouds, aircraft went into a spin. In righting the plane, could see ocean waves below – too close!

21st May, sunrise: Fuel leak in cockpit. Exhaust flames could set light to fuel. Will land as soon as possible.

21st May, early afternoon: Flying over Ireland. No airfield in sight.

Arrive in Culmore, Northern Ireland, 21st May 1932.

Made it!

Moo!

Where am I?

In Gallagher's pasture.

Have you come far?

Just from America!

1st June 1937, Miami, Florida …

Amelia and navigator Fred Noonan plan to fly around the world. Could this be Amelia's greatest challenge yet?

29th June 1937: Amelia lands in New Guinea to refuel.

We've flown 22 000 miles already. There are only 7000 to go, but I'm totally exhausted and not feeling well.

We'll need to land on Howland Island to refuel next.

It'll be tough to hit it – our navigation will have to be perfect. If not, we'll run out of fuel …

Amelia and Fred Noonan took off for Howland Island on 1st July 1937.

They never reached the island and their aircraft was never found.

The whole world was shocked when Amelia disappeared.

Amelia was a great pioneer. She proved that women could be just as brave, tough and clever as men.

Amelia Earhart facts

Amelia Earhart
American aviator
24th July 1897–
2nd July 1937

- Amelia was born on 24th July, 1894 in Kansas, USA.
- She is known for two major achievements: first woman to fly across the Atlantic Ocean and first solo transatlantic flight.
- She was a popular figure with people all over the world. The US Post Office issued the Amelia Earhart commemorative airmail stamp on her birthday many years after her death, in 1963.
- Amelia died on 2nd July 1937, when her aircraft disappeared over the Pacific Ocean. The US government spent $4 million searching for Amelia afterwards but with no success.
- In her own words: "My ambition is to have this wonderful gift produce practical results for the future of commercial flying and for the women who may want to fly tomorrow's planes."

Frank Whittle

Amelia was a real pioneer of flight, but global air travel would be a lot slower today without our next pioneer.

Royal Air Force Training College, Cranwell, UK, 1927...

Do you fancy going to the pictures, Frank?

No thanks – I'm working on something.

Frank's obsessed with aircraft design. He thinks planes could fly much faster.

Sounds like he's a dreamer!

Sir, I've been working on ideas for new aircraft engines.

Hmm, let me look.

It works by mixing air and fuel at very high temperatures.

That's brilliant! You should show it to the Air Ministry.

At the Air Ministry...

The Air Force needs clever chaps like you, but this simply wouldn't work.

But, Sir, have you looked ...

Run along and stop wasting my time!

This is the future! If only they could see it.

"I think we can raise the money to make my engine work."

"This turbojet is more powerful than anything ever built before."

12th April 1937, Rugby, UK ...

"The engine will turn at 8000 revolutions per minute, Mr Whittle."

"That's good, but not good enough. Back to the drawing board, boys!"

"It's running at 13 000 **RPM**. I think we've done it!"

Suddenly ...

Boom!

"We've rebuilt the engine with ten separate chambers so it's much more reliable."

"Let's hope so. We'll soon be at war with Germany and they may have got hold of your early plans ..."

After the outbreak of World War Two in 1939, more engineers joined Frank's team in the race to build the first jet aircraft.

On 15th May 1941, RAF Cranwell ...

"This is it, the moment of truth."

"Frank, it flies!"

"Well, that's what it was designed for, isn't it?"

"How does it work? It's got no propeller."

"It's easy, old boy – it just sucks itself along like a vacuum cleaner."

"The test was a success."

"We need a jet fighter in the sky now. Make sure our allies in the USA get copies of the plans."

General Electric Company, USA ...

"We're all thrilled to be working on this project. Jets are the future of flying."

"I wish someone had said that fifteen years ago!"

The Gloster Meteor first flew in 1944. This jet fighter was used to attack V-1 flying bombs that were targeting British cities.

"Today's jet aircraft that carry passengers around the world are all based on Frank's work."

"Imagine a world without aircraft like these ..."

Frank Whittle facts

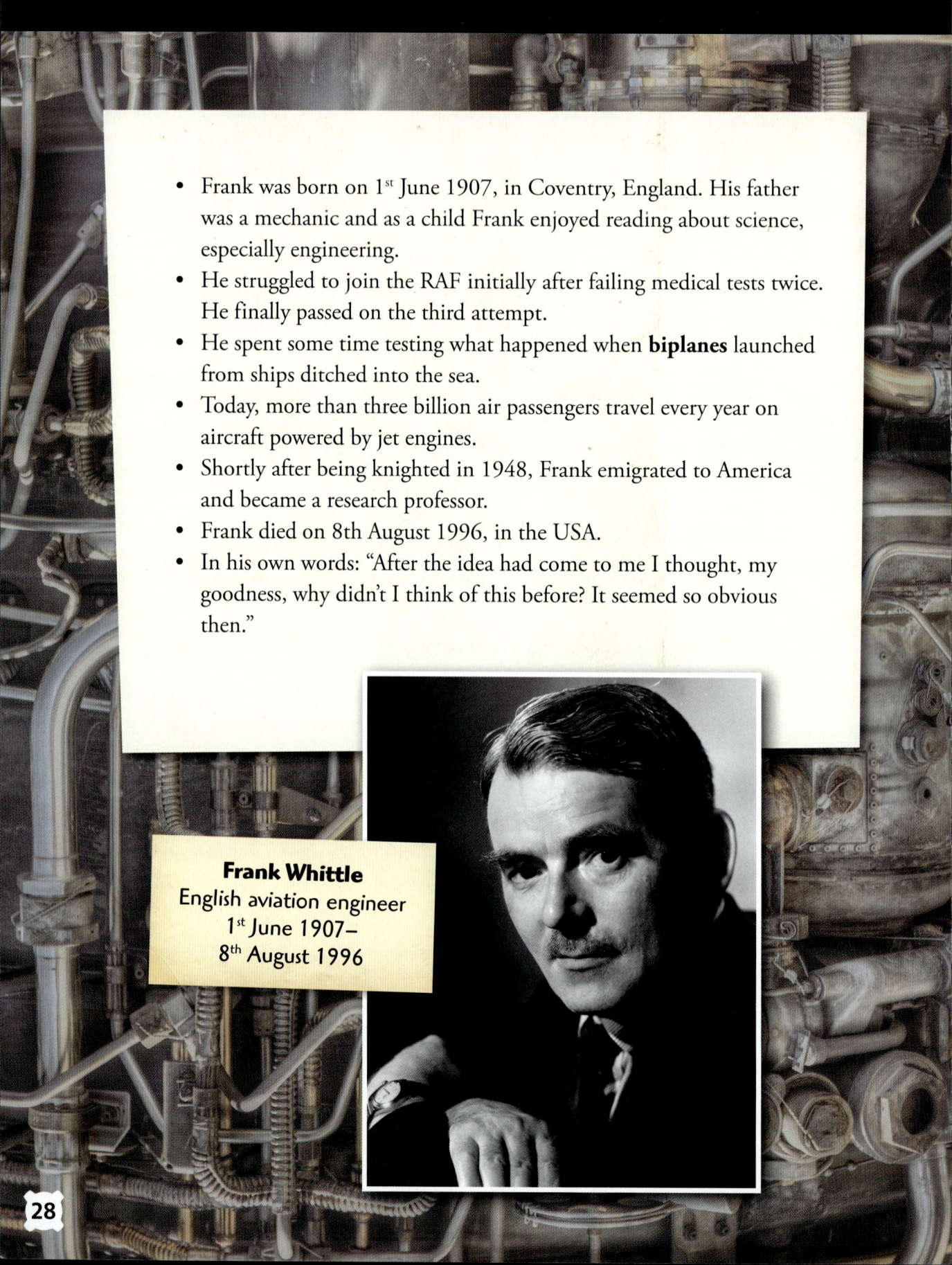

- Frank was born on 1st June 1907, in Coventry, England. His father was a mechanic and as a child Frank enjoyed reading about science, especially engineering.
- He struggled to join the RAF initially after failing medical tests twice. He finally passed on the third attempt.
- He spent some time testing what happened when **biplanes** launched from ships ditched into the sea.
- Today, more than three billion air passengers travel every year on aircraft powered by jet engines.
- Shortly after being knighted in 1948, Frank emigrated to America and became a research professor.
- Frank died on 8th August 1996, in the USA.
- In his own words: "After the idea had come to me I thought, my goodness, why didn't I think of this before? It seemed so obvious then."

Frank Whittle
English aviation engineer
1st June 1907–
8th August 1996

Clarence Birdseye

This pioneer shows that very simple ideas can make a big difference.

Clarence Birdseye grew up in an age of invention. New inventions kept appearing ...

... like the motor car ...

... the escalator ...

What makes it go?

... the **phonograph** to record and play music ...

How does it make music?

... and the lightweight camera.

Where does the picture come from?

When he was old enough, Clarence went to university ...

Hi. What are you studying?

I study everything, but mostly science.

What's in that bag?

Frogs. I'm selling them to the zoo for the snakes to eat.

Clarence loved finding unusual ways to make money.

29

When he left university, he went looking for adventure.

Clarence travelled in the American wilderness.

"What's cooking, Birdseye?"

"Field mouse and chipmunk stew."

"Yuck! I'll stick to canned vegetables."

In 1912, Labrador, Canada ...

"Wow, this is cold!"

"This is spring. You wait until winter."

Clarence stayed in frozen Labrador for five years. He married Eleanor Gannett while living there.

"What's for dinner?"

"Fish ... There's not much else."

"What do you do with all your fish?"

"They freeze in the cold air. We cook them later."

"This tastes as good as fresh fish. I wonder why?"

30

Clarence realized that the fish stayed fresh because they were frozen almost instantly. By chance, his next job was all about fish.
If we could keep fish fresh for people living far from the sea, we would sell more fish.
U.S. FISHERIES ASSOCIATION
What are you doing?
I've made a fish-freezing breakthrough!
Clarence left his job. Frozen fish was the future for him.
U.S. FISHERIES ASSOCIATION
Inside this building is a miracle of fish-freezing technology!
I just need a bit more investment.
Birdseye Seafoods
Hmm, I'm not sure ...
I can't borrow any more money. What can we do?

Clarence and his wife sold their house and put the money into the business ... it was a big risk to take.

1925, Gloucester, Massachusetts ...

This town is our new home. In our factory by the harbour we'll change food forever!

Clarence experimented with freezing all kinds of fish, vegetables and meat. He even froze an alligator!

This grocery store says they have nowhere cold to store our frozen food.

We've got a warehouse full of food that no one can buy.

Whose yacht is that?

Marjorie Merriweather Post – the food millionaire.

Where did you get this delicious fresh goose?

The frozen food factory sent it.

Later ...

With your brains and my money, this frozen food could make you rich and me even richer!

Clarence sold the company to Mrs Post's General Foods. Soon, frozen food really took off. However, Clarence hadn't finished inventing ...

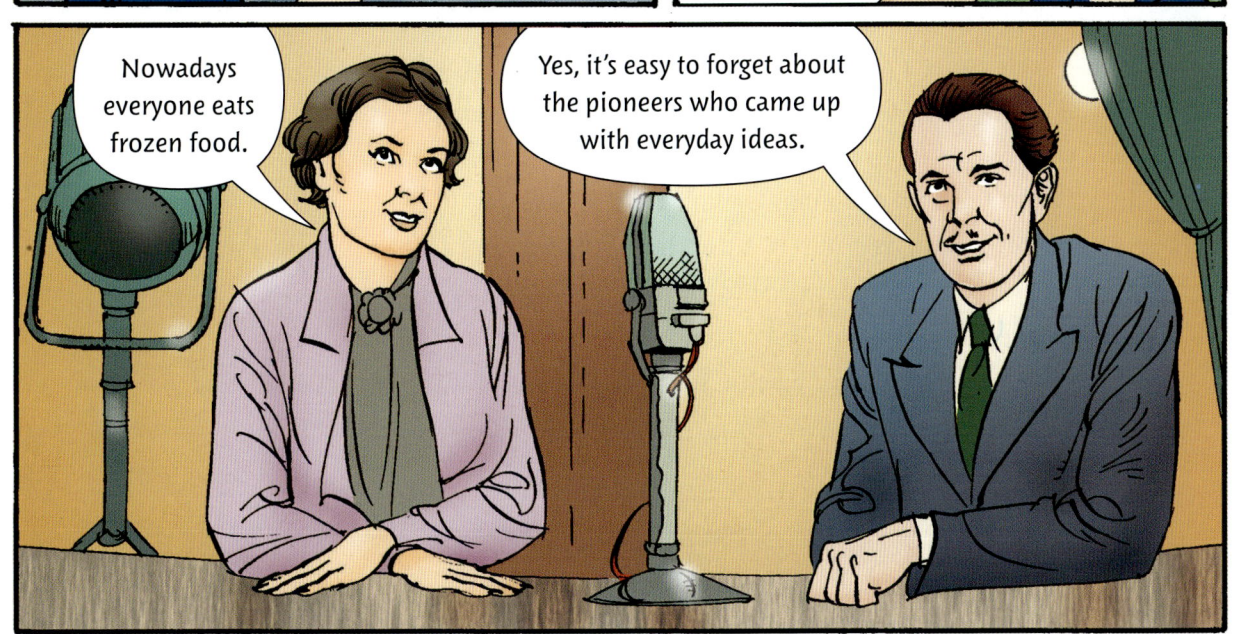

"These new light bulbs include a reflector to make them brighter."

"Another brilliant idea, Mr Birdseye!"

"What are you working on today, Mr Birdseye?"

"Dried food! I'm using heat and air to take water out of these carrots."

"Will it work?"

"I'll keep trying until it does!"

"Nowadays everyone eats frozen food."

"Yes, it's easy to forget about the pioneers who came up with everyday ideas."

33

Clarence Birdseye facts

Clarence Birdseye
American inventor
9th December 1886–
7th October 1956

- Clarence was born on 9th December 1886, in New York, USA, the sixth of nine children.
- He had wanted to become a biologist but had to give up university due to lack of funds. However, his first job was in a related field and involved removing ticks from small mammals in Montana, USA!
- He worked tirelessly trying to find the very best way to freeze food to retain its original flavour and texture.
- In total, he registered more than 300 **patents** for new inventions, from heat lamps to fishing equipment.
- Clarence died on 7th October, 1956.
- In his own words: "To be perfectly honest, I am best described as just a guy with a very large bump of curiosity."

Jacques Piccard

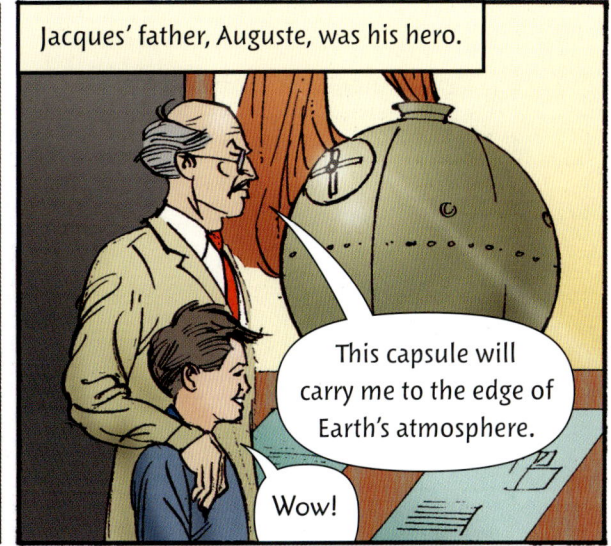

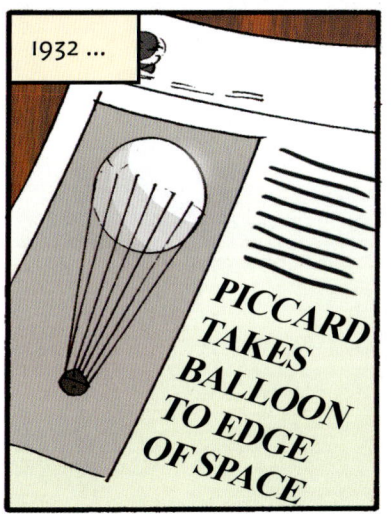

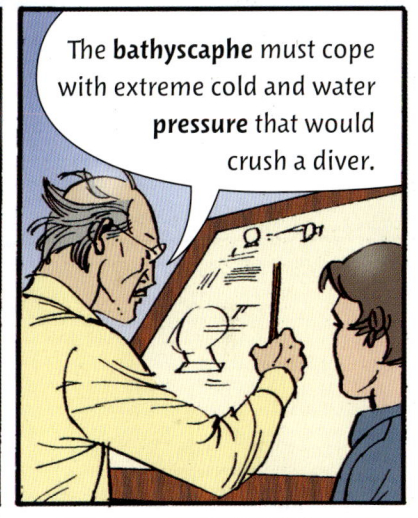

Our next pioneer is more interested in conserving fish rather than catching and freezing them!

Jacques' father, Auguste, was his hero.

This capsule will carry me to the edge of Earth's atmosphere.

Wow!

1932 ...

PICCARD TAKES BALLOON TO EDGE OF SPACE

1942 ...

I want to explore new places.

Then help with my new project to explore the oceans.

The **bathyscaphe** must cope with extreme cold and water **pressure** that would crush a diver.

1953, while testing the bathyscaphe *Trieste* ...

This capsule is so strong. We could take it many kilometres underwater.

Maybe, but you need a younger co-pilot, Jacques. I'm too old for this. You should take over developing the *Trieste* further.

The US Navy wants to use the *Trieste* for research. I can help and do some real exploring.

35

Panel 1:
- Would you sell the *Trieste* to us? You could still pilot it.
- OK, on one condition …

Panel 2:
- I want to go to the deepest point on Earth – the **Challenger Deep** in the Pacific Ocean. I need you to help with support ships and crew.
- OK. Don Walsh will be your co-pilot.

Panel 3:
23rd January 1960, 8am …
- Some instruments have been damaged by the waves, Jacques.
- It's perfectly safe, Don. We dive today.

TRIESTE US NAVY

Panel 4:
- Control are worried that the *Trieste* may be unsafe because of the damage.

Panel 5:
- Tell them the *Trieste* is already 7000 metres down.
- But it's not.
- It will be soon.

Panel 6:
- We're on our way.

Panel 7:
- It's getting cold.

36

Depth of 7000 metres (23 000 feet) ...

No one's ever been deeper than this.

Crack!

What was that? Have we hit bottom?

Not yet. Should we go back?

No – we can do it!

Depth of 10911 metres (35 800 feet) ...

We're on the seabed!

We made it!

I think I can see a fish. So life can survive down here!

That fish has never seen light before!

I don't want to worry you but I think I know what that noise was ...

Let's get going. Only seven miles to go – we'll be back in about four hours.

What a relief ... that cracked window was just strong enough.

TRIESTE
US NAVY

37

Two years later ...
If only more people could find out about life deep underwater.
How could we do that?
I'll invent a submarine for tourists, with windows.
Welcome to my underwater tour of Lake Geneva!
In 1969, Jacques drifted his new submarine 3000 kilometres under the Atlantic Ocean.
In 1999, Jacques' son, Bertrand, piloted the first non-stop balloon flight around the world.
I wouldn't have gone on so many expeditions if I knew how hard it was for those left behind awaiting news!
The Piccards are an amazing family of pioneers. They managed to go higher, deeper and further than anyone before them.

Jacques Piccard facts

Jacques Piccard
Swiss oceanic engineer
28th July 1922–
1st November 2008

- Jacques was born on 28th July 1922 in Brussels, Belgium.
- He interrupted his university studies to serve in the French Army in World War Two.
- It was to be over fifty years before another person reached the Challenger Deep, showing what an achievement it was.
- He made his last dive aged 82.
- Jacques died on 1st November 2008, in Switzerland.
- In his own words: "There is a driving force in all of us, which cannot stop if there is still one step beyond."

Nelson Mandela

This pioneer has got to be one of the greatest of all.

On 10th May 1994, Nelson was sworn in as the first black president of South Africa.

Nelson Mandela is a hero in South Africa and around the world.

I have walked that long road to freedom ...

However, for much of his life he was treated like a criminal.

On his first day at school, Rolihlahla Mandela was given a new name ...

Your British name is Nelson.

Black people were treated as second-class citizens in South Africa.

Although most South Africans were black, white people ran the government and made the laws.

WHITES ONLY

Nelson went to Fort Hare, South Africa, one of the only colleges that accepted black students.

They say we are Africa's future leaders.

But we will still not be equal to white South Africans.

40

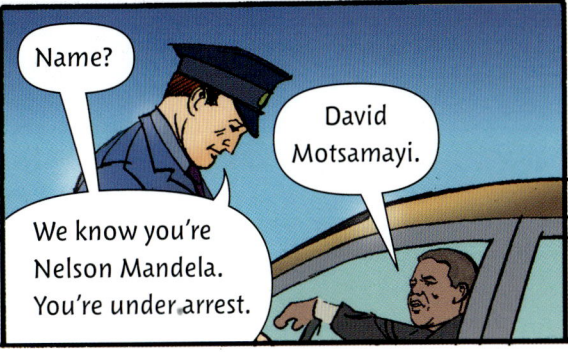

In 1944, Nelson joined the **African National Congress** (ANC). This group wanted equal rights for black South Africans.

"We are born in African-Only hospitals and we live in African-Only areas. We must change this."

But in 1948 things became worse …

"They've changed the law to keep all races separate. They call it **apartheid**."

"We must protest and strike for equal rights."

Nelson and other ANC members faced arrest and prison for protesting against apartheid.

In 1961, after a long trial, Nelson was freed.

"Not guilty."

He went into hiding to avoid being arrested again, but continued to protest.

"You're a wanted man."

"I travel at night, using different names, not staying in one place too long."

"We are always under attack."

"Name?"

"David Motsamayi."

"We know you're Nelson Mandela. You're under arrest."

41

"These men were part of a plot to overthrow the government."

"In June 1964, Nelson was sentenced to spend the rest of his life in prison."

"Robben Island Prison, near Cape Town ..."

"Move!"

"Robben Island was to be Nelson's home for eighteen years."

"Prisoners were forced to do back-breaking work."

"While he was imprisoned, Nelson's fame spread around the world."

FREE MANDELA

FREE MANDELA

"In 1985, now in Pollsmoor Prison ..."

"There is growing pressure on the government to change. They will release you if you speak out against violence."

"I cannot make any deals unless I am free."

In 1990, President F.W. de Klerk realized that South Africa had to change ...
The time for negotiation has arrived.
Nelson was freed at last ... but there was still a lot of work for him to do.
Today the majority of South Africans, black and white, recognize that apartheid has no future.
Now we can start to create an undivided South Africa.
27th April 1994, South Africa's first election since the end of apartheid.
Today, I'm casting the first vote in my life.
South Africans lined up to vote.
POLLING STATION
Nelson was their choice as South Africa's new president.
I swear to devote myself to the well-being of the Republic and all its people.

"This is a time to heal the old wounds and build a new South Africa."

Nelson's wish to unite South Africa was shown by his support for the country's rugby team. Rugby was mainly played by white South Africans.

President Mandela tried to tackle poverty and the lack of education caused by many years of apartheid.

"Nelson Mandela was a true pioneer for human rights."

"He was an inspiration to many as he forgave the people who put him in prison."

Nelson Mandela facts

- Nelson was born on 18th July 1918, in Mvezo, a village in South Africa's Eastern Cape.
- His original name was Rolihlahla. In the Xhosa language this means troublemaker, or literally 'pulling the branch of a tree'.
- In 2009, the United Nations voted to mark 18th July every year as Mandela Day, to celebrate the life and influence of this great pioneer.
- As well as the Nobel Peace Prize, he has many other awards including over fifty honorary degrees from universities across the world.
- Nelson died on 5th December 2013, at his home in Johannesburg, South Africa.
- In his own words: "What counts in life is not the mere fact that we have lived. It is what difference we have made to the lives of others that will determine the significance of the life we lead."

Nelson Mandela
South African civil rights activist and president
18th July 1918–
5th December 2013

More great pioneers

This book has included all sorts of pioneers, from inventors to leaders and aviators.

But these are just a few of the amazing pioneers from our past. Here are some more inspiring people ...

Mohandas Gandhi

Mohandas was the leader of the campaign for Indian independence in the 1940s. He was a peaceful leader who believed in non-violent protest and was known for fasting as a form of social protest.

Edmund Hillary and Tenzing Norgay

On 29th May 1953, the New Zealand-born Edmund Hilary and the Nepalese Tenzing Norgay became the first climbers to reach the summit of Mount Everest. The climb from base camp to the summit took over two months.

Coco Chanel

Coco Chanel was a French fashion designer famous for designing clothes for women that didn't rely on corsets, something that was unheard of at the time. Her clothes became popular after World War One, and her legacy as a designer lives on today.

Sir Ludwig Guttmann

Sir Ludwig Guttmann was a doctor and director of the National Spinal Injuries Centre. In 1948 he organized the very first Paralympic Games at the centre to tie in with the London Olympics that same year.

Sirimavo Bandaranaike

Sirimavo Bandaranaike was the world's first elected female prime minister. She served as Prime Minister of Ceylon and Sri Lanka a total of three times between 1960 and 2000.

Wangari Maathai

Wangari Maathai was a Kenyan environmental campaigner and political activist. In the 1970s she founded the Green Belt Movement which worked alongside the UN to employ women to plant seeds, combating deforestation and allowing many poor women to earn their own money.

Kay Cottee

Kay Cottee became the first woman to sail non-stop around the world, single-handed, in 1988. The voyage took her 189 days, and she was washed overboard at one point in the journey.

Barack Obama

Barack Obama made history in 2009 when he became the first African American President of the USA.

Malala Yousafzai

Malala Yousafzai from Pakistan is a campaigner for education and women's rights. In 2014 she became the youngest ever winner of the Nobel Peace Prize.

Glossary

African National Congress	a political party that led the struggle to end apartheid in South Africa (ANC)
altimeter	a device that shows how high above sea level an aircraft is flying
apartheid	the political system in South Africa that distinguished between people of different races and did not give equal rights to non-white people
bathyscaphe	a vehicle for exploring ocean depths, which uses a float to lower and raise itself in the water
biplane	a plane with two sets of wings, attached one above the other
Challenger Deep	the deepest point on Earth, in the Mariana Trench of the Pacific Ocean
hunger strike	a protest in which a person refuses to eat anything for long periods
navigation	a way of making sure that you, or your ship or aircraft, are going in the right direction
patent	an official document that registers an invention so no one else can copy it
phonograph	a machine to record and play sound, invented by Thomas Edison
pressure	the force that pushes against something, such as air or water pressure
RPM	a way of measuring how many times a wheel turns in a minute; RPM stands for 'revolutions per minute'
suffragette	a woman who took part in protests to try and gain the right to vote

Index

aircraft engines 24–27
aeroplanes 16–22, 26–27
Alexandra Palace 6
apartheid 41, 43, 44
Atlantic Ocean, the 18
British Broadcasting Corporation, the (BBC) 4–6
broadcasting 6–7
flying 16–22, 24–27
frozen foods 31–33
Queen Victoria 9
prison 10–13, 15, 41–42, 44
Royal Air Force, the (RAF) 24, 26
suffragettes 10–14
television 4–7
voting 14, 43
Women's Social and Political Union, the (WSPU) 10